Quotes About Living

by Doe Zantamata

Written by Doe Zantamata

Edited by Doe Zantamata

Website:

www.happinessinyourlife.com

Blogs:

www.QuotesAboutLiving.com

www.thehiyL.com

ISBN-9781491010341

Independently Published.

This book is dedicated to everyone
who has become a part of
Happiness in Your Life
since 2011.

Contents

1. Karma

Karma is a word often used as a curse on those who have done someone wrong. It's also thought of as a way that someone will receive payback for good or bad that they've done. Karma is not a punishment or reward system. It is based on understanding. If you only do good things in expectation of reward, the reward will not show up. If you do good things purely for the basis of helping another, then it will show up without fail. Karma is not something that can be controlled, but it is something that always delivers.

Encouraging people to live their own truths is a great gift. Encouraging someone to live your truth is a huge burden.

If you do something nice for someone with no expectation of anything in return and they question you as to why you are doing it, or ask, "What's in it for you?" don't take offense. They can only see what's in themselves in the world. They've just told you that they wouldn't do anything nice for someone unless there was something in it for them. But also, if someone accepts gratefully with no question, they've just told you that they also would do nice things with no expectation of anything in return.

As you allow flow and change to occur and as you keep looking inward, letting go of situations that cause you grief and increasing the amount of time spent in situations that allow you to be happy, your world will change.

No matter how much you regret, how angry or sad you become, your yesterdays will never return. The world of "should have," "could have," or "if only would have" is a world of pointless suffering.

Many people love to give. It's a great feeling, and they do so with no expectation. But they are often awful at receiving, and really deprive others of that joy of giving. If given a gift, they say, "You shouldn't have," "It's too much," or the worst, "I feel bad that you got me this." Ouch. This creates bad feelings during what should be a nice moment, and though their intent was to be selfless and polite, it is actually ungrateful. When a gift is given, "thank you" says that they appreciate the time, consideration, and effort that person has already put forth. Giving is virtuous, but so is accepting gratefully.

Be careful of the Karma of Judgment. When you say, "How could anyone..." or "I can't understand why someone would..." you are literally asking the universe to give you that experience. Karma isn't about punishment or reward, it's about understanding. When you judge someone, you will soon find yourself in a similar position as they were. You will then see why they made the seemingly bad choices they made, and you may even make the exact same ones. If not, at least you'll know why they did.

Every single day holds opportunities for growth. If you're seeing something negative persist in your life, picture a goal of what you'd ideally like that picture to look like instead. Keep that picture fresh in your mind daily, and make choices that are in the direction of that picture. If something or someone does not fit into that picture, then put your attention on someone or something that does instead.

There are 12 Laws of Karma.

LAW I – THE GREAT LAW

As you sow, so shall you reap. You have complete control over all your actions, and absolutely no control over many of the consequences. Eventually, however, all of your good actions will lead to good consequences.

LAW II – THE LAW OF CREATION

Almost identical to the Law of Attraction, this law states that "You attract what you are, not what you want." This follows also closely to, "You can judge a person by the company he keeps," or "Birds of a feather flock together." You surround yourself with people and circumstances that reflect your beliefs about yourself and the world.

LAW III ⸗ THE LAW OF HUMILITY

"What you resist, persists for you." The energy of something that you don't want cannot be cleared or changed by you expending more of that same energy. In order to see more good, you must do more good.

LAW IV – THE LAW OF GROWTH

"Wherever you go, there you are." Your surroundings are representative of the beliefs you hold about yourself and the world. As you grow, you make different choices. With those different choices come different consequences. If you want to change your world, change yourself – the cause – and your world will change, effortlessly. This does go the other way. If a person goes through a traumatic experience and allows that experience to dominate their beliefs, eventually they will "lose everything," their job, their home, their spouse and their outer world will represent what their beliefs are inside.

LAW V – THE LAW OF MIRRORS

When people insult you, don't take offense, don't take it personally, but do listen to their words. They are telling you how they see the world, and they are telling you the exact negative qualities they possess. The Fifth Law of Karma, "The Law of Mirrors" states that one can only see what's in them, regardless if it is what is actually present in reality or not. Release the need to defend or try to explain to them that you're not being whatever-nasty-insult-they've-thrown-at-you, but evaluate instead all of these insults, and realize that this is who they are. Then, decide if a person with those qualities is one who you'd like in your life or not.

If they can see it in you and label it, but you can't see it, it's not in you.

If you can see it in them and label it, but they can't see it, it's not in them.

If you both can see and label it, it's in both of you...good or bad.

LAW VI – THE LAW OF SYNCHRONICITY

"Whatever you do may seem unimportant, but it is very important that you do it." Everything and everyone in this world is connected. Every little good act builds another in some way, and every harsh act creates another in some way. The energy created within an individual may seem tiny and insignificant when sent out, but it will continue to ripple and build in one way or another through every person it touches.

LAW VII – THE LAW OF DIRECTION AND MOTIVES

The Seventh Law is also called "The Law of Focus." It states that your mind cannot be in two places at once. When faced with a tragedy or loss, our immediate reaction is usually sadness or anger. As we grieve, our mind naturally seeks the positive. It is our choice if we want to continue to grieve for the rest of our days, or if we want to move past the pain, and be grateful for the experience. Even if the entire experience was painful, we can still be grateful for the lesson, and for the fact that it is over.

LAW VIII – THE LAW OF WILLINGNESS

This law states in part that what you believe to be true, the universe will demonstrate that truth to you. When negative outer circumstances challenge your positive beliefs, just hold on to your beliefs and don't let those temporary negative influences change them. If you do change your beliefs to negative ones, the universe will then switch to show you more negative. Keep believing in positive, and the universe will then turn that something that seemed negative into something positive.

LAW IX – THE LAW OF BE HERE NOW

This law states, "You can't go home again, but you must try." Home means your emotional home. The starting point you were as a child, when you believed in love, trusted fully, and believed in the good in people. Years of pain and bad experience can cause a person to become bitter and to change their beliefs to ones that are self-centered, mistrusting, and withholding of love in an attempt at protecting themselves from pain. But to live in that space is to live in a constant state of pain. Freeing oneself from that prison is up to the individual.

LAW X – THE LAW OF CHANGE

The Tenth Law of Karma is "The Law of Change." It states that if you want change, you must start inside yourself. If you are unhappy with something or someone in your life, only ending a relationship with them will not solve the problem. They will just show up again in your life with a different name and a different face. Do you know a person who goes from one bad relationship to another? Are you that person? Remember, the outside world is just a mirror. To have change occur, it must begin with you.

LAW XI – THE LAW OF PATIENCE AND REWARD

What you focus on increases. Don't compare you life to others, don't look at everything in your life that you are lacking. Look instead to the things you have; the good in your life. Separate your mind from negative events. Continue to do your best and move forward. Eventually, everything will work out in your favor, even if it doesn't appear so today.

LAW XII – THE LAW OF VALUE AND UPLIFTMENT

The great things you contribute may not be reflected right back to you, but they do increase the collective good. By doing your best, you increase in your way, the value of the whole. Certain people throughout history have awakened in millions truth, freedom, peace, and compassion. In and of themselves, their lives may not have been opulent or easy, but the value they added to millions upon millions of lives is immeasurable.

2. Intuition

Intuition literally means learning from within. Most of us were not taught how to use this sense, but all of us know that "gut" feeling. Learn to trust your inner feeling and it will become stronger. Avoid going against your better judgment or getting talked into things that just don't feel right.

Intuition is a sense, just like sight or touch, or any other sense. Some people have a stronger sense of intuition, just like some people have incredible hearing. Some people take the time to train their intuition, as most of us were trained to use our other senses when we were children. There is no magic to it. Hearing uses sound, sight uses three-dimensional images, and intuition uses energy. Training and using your intuition is as valuable as using any other sense, and without it, you're missing part of the world.

As you learn to trust and act on your sense of intuition, it will continue to strengthen. Soon, it will become like any other sense, and will guide you toward good and away from danger. If you saw a train coming toward you, you would move out of the way. If you hear the phone, you answer it. This will become the way your intuition works. You will "just know" when to move toward or away from people and circumstances, as reliably as if you saw, heard, or knew with information from any other sense.

Intuition has two distinct differences from the other senses:

1. It is only a guide for most people, which points in one direction, towards or away from.

2. It is the only sense that is not confirmed in the present moment, but rather the confirmation will take place in the future.

These two key differences are likely the reason why it's questioned as a sense by many people.

Your intuition is a sense that's been given to you not to ignore, but to use and help you navigate through life. Trust your intuition. If it feels wrong, it probably is.

Intuition is the only sense that our minds argue with. Maybe it's because it isn't globally accepted as a sense yet, but things sure do change when we see it for what it is.

Can you imagine arguing with other senses? What you'd miss, what you'd do and wouldn't?

It seems silly, but it would be like hearing the phone ring and thinking, "that phone's not really ringing." Or seeing a car driving straight towards you and thinking, "hmm, I see a car coming straight towards me but maybe I ought to just stand here anyway."

People who learn to trust and use their intuition are still going to have negative experiences in their lives. This does not mean that their intuition failed them. Intuition is always right.

Some of these experiences hold very important lessons for us, which we may only see when looking back years later. During the difficult time, using your intuition will help to guide you through them in the best way possible.

Intuition comes in many forms. One way that often happens is a jolt to a stop. This happens when a trigger is set off in you that feels like a threat to either your self-worth or your survival centers. Think of an exaggerated example. If you were walking in the woods and suddenly spotted a bear a few yards away looking right at you. Your body would freeze, stiffen, and straighten. If in any daily circumstance, you feel this within, pause and try to identify what caused it. Is it a real threat or a trigger that is familiar to a past threat but has no real relation to today? Intuition will let you know that something is amiss, but then it's up to your mind to process and figure out what exactly it means to you.

You can never make a full decision on only a little information. But most times, all the information's not all readily right there for you to see. This is where your intuition helps a lot. If you're feeling a lot of hesitation but logically it sounds fine, then it may not be something to dive into. If you're feeling drawn to it, then either it's the right thing or there's a lesson in it that a part of you wants to learn. In uncertainty, stay very aware of your feelings throughout the day. If the feelings are more heavy than expansive, it may be something you let go without having to find out what those feelings were indicating early on. If you have a lot of really good feelings inside even though doubts may enter your mind later, then going with it is probably a much better road to follow.

Let your intuition be your guide, but keep your mind alert to process what that sense is telling you.

Intuition is the intelligence of the heart and the knowledge of the soul. It knows instantly and constantly what can take decades of experience for the mind to logically sort out and understand. Trust it, and the reason will follow in time.

You can spend your life looking out, making decisions and having reactions to people and things you see. Or, you can spend your life looking in, staying in close contact with how you feel in any given moment, responding to those feelings to encourage more of the peaceful ones. If you choose the first, it seems like you're trying to connect with the world, but if you choose the second, you actually do.

Only you know in your heart what feels best for you. Trust yourself and your innermost intelligence. If the choice is to disappoint another person with the truth or disappoint yourself with trying to deny the truth, find the courage to disappoint them. It will only be short term. In the long run, the real disappointment would be for them to find out your heart was never there. But by then it will be too late and neither of you will be able to relive a life that's really true.

One incredibly important thing to always, always remember about intuition is the tie between intuition and energy.

There are only two methods of action;

1. Destruction, and

2. Construction.

Intuition will never, ever, ever be a feeling, thought, have signs, or anything towards destructive behavior.

Destructive behavior includes following, forcing, controlling, restricting, stalking, harming, holding a person against their will or killing a person. These are all fear based actions that fall under the false belief that if a person is in some way controlled or "gotten rid of," then somehow things would be better. Will this ever apply to you? I hope not. But in the news media, some of the most heinous and violent crimes against children, against organizations, or against entire cultures is done with the belief of the offender that "God told them to do it" and that the world would be better if they did. Even John Wilkes Booth thought that his assassination of Abraham Lincoln was going to be considered a heroic act.

If you or anyone you know are ever indicating that some kind of voice is telling you or them that a group of people is evil, or "must be stopped" or expresses a hatred that sets off your inner alarm bells, don't wait until energy is added to that and it grows. Don't pass it off or think they are joking. So many of the tragedies that occur could have been prevented if only warning signs were not ignored. If it turns out they were joking or you were overreacting or got them in trouble for no reason, those are much lesser offenses than letting something awful happen that cannot ever be repaired.

3. Forgiveness

Anyone can hold a grudge, but it takes a person with character to forgive. When you forgive, you release yourself from a painful burden. Forgiveness doesn't mean what happened was OK, and it doesn't mean that person should still be welcome in your life. It just means you have made peace with the pain, and are ready to let it go.

Forgiveness only means to let go of resentment towards a person or event. It means to accept that it happened, and to move on from there. It does not mean to pretend that it never happened at all.

How do you make peace with pain? If it were towards a person, a time in life, or an entire childhood, recognize first that you can be grateful that time is over. What remains today is a memory. If 10 years were spent living in that pain, know that this day forward, you get to live without it. Keep your mind in the present. See the positives. Today is better than any of those days, and you appreciate good people more due to it. There were lessons in there that you never have to learn again. You are here. Now, you are truly free to live.

Forgiveness to another says, "I love myself more than I dislike your actions towards me."

Forgiveness to self says, "I love and accept that I am not perfect. I release regret, and know that now, and in the future, I will not repeat the actions which caused me to feel this regret. I can do nothing to bring back yesterday, but this lesson has changed all tomorrows."

Forgive in love, be grateful for the lesson, and be free.

Choosing forgiveness doesn't mean that the wounds will suddenly vanish. All healing; physical, emotional, and mental, takes time. Choosing forgiveness means that you've decided to begin the healing process.

Instead of thinking, "I will not forgive that person because..." shift it to, "I choose to hold on to the resentment of that pain because..."

How does holding on to that pain really help your life?

What benefit is there for you to keep it alive?

Once you make that shift inside, you will always find reason to forgive, and will never find reason not to. The key benefit to forgiving is the freedom to love and trust again.

One of the biggest obstacles to forgiveness is dealing with loss. There is something lost, that sometimes might be able to be regained, but most often, is lost forever. Forgiveness means first, acceptance of how things are today. Not how they might have been if only that person acted differently, but how they really are today. Once you can focus your attention onto what you do have today, not what you no longer have, you have made a giant leap towards true forgiveness.

Forgiveness requires strength, and the ability to see that the true benefit is for your own happiness. If someone stole from you, holding resentment won't bring your things back, but it will keep anger alive in your heart. If you were cheated on or deceived, holding on to anger won't make that person any more honest or undo anything that's been done, but it will keep a place in your heart imprisoned. Allowing past anger to exist in the present will damage or limit new relationships.

Forgive yourself for not knowing what you didn't know
before you learned it.

The Forgiveness Difference:

People who don't forgive say,

"I cannot accomplish something BECAUSE OF that person."

They feel that person or circumstance ruined them in some way and made them incapable of some good, desirable thing in life...a job, a loving relationship, happiness.

People who forgive say,

"I can accomplish something REGARDLESS of that person."

They feel that person or circumstance happened, but now it's over. Life can go on. They are still just as capable as they were before of good, desirable things in life. They do not let that person affect them anymore. They take control of their own life and their own happiness, and do not allow another person to rob them of great things that life has in store for them.

Forgiving yourself is a gift to the world. If you can look at your own mistakes and see them as mistakes of a good person, you'll develop compassion. You'll be able to look at others and see that they are good people who also made mistakes. If you believe you are a bad or stupid person, you won't believe you can contribute much to the world. Believing you are good and wiser for your mistakes will allow you to contribute wisdom, compassion, and forgiveness in your time here, making it a kinder and more forgiving place...and that's exactly what the world needs.

If you think about how many times you've been lied to, taken advantage of or not appreciated, you'll likely not even want to get out of bed. But if you think about how much life you have ahead of you, how many beautiful experiences await you in the weeks and years ahead, you can rise with optimism and walk with wisdom. Those other experiences didn't break you, they taught you the value of kindness and honesty and that what you give to the world is so rare it's sometimes not believed. You don't have to be a victim or a martyr or even a survivor. Just be a wiser version of your former self.

Compassionate reflection allows you to see yourself from a different perspective. As time passes, the person you become will detach from yet understand the person you were. Choices and circumstances can then be viewed as they were, accepted as how they were, and negative emotion can be released.

4. Trust

You are not a fool for trusting someone who lied to you. They are the fool for lying to someone who trusted them. It's the easiest thing in the world to get away with temporarily, and the hardest thing to recover from permanently. Please don't let it change you. There are already way too many of them and far too few of you.

Trust is as necessary to a happy, healthy relationship as air is to the lungs. With it, a relationship can survive almost anything. Without it, almost nothing.

Living in a world without trust is truly painful. When a person says, "trust is something that needs to be earned," it's a big sign that this person's trust was broken one too many times, and they got fed up. Without trust, stories are invented, and drama flows freely. With trust, a person can take people's word at face value, not read into things negatively, and just be happier. It was not up to you to be lied to, but it is up to you to trust again.

When we are young, we trust fully. We even believe in the Easter Bunny or Tooth Fairy, just because we're told they exist. At some point, we find out about lies. At first, lying comes as a shock, but many come to accept it as a "normal" way of life. To trust, you have to have faith in the best of people. After your trust is broken many times, you may think that by not trusting, or by being skeptical, you'll not be fooled. But the true fool is the one who chooses to mistrust, as it never, ever, leads to happiness.

It's never a good time for bad news, but it's always the right time for the truth. The longer a lie is held, the more difficult it becomes to reveal the truth. If it's held a long time, two truths must be told; the original lie, and the reason it was held and covered so many times for so long. One becomes a thousand, and one is easier to forgive, and maintain trust, than many. Revealing is painful, but sooner is always easier, less painful, and better than later.

First bliss comes naturally. Second bliss is a choice. It's the choice to trust, to love, to put yourself out there, knowing full well that you can get hurt. But you won't be able to live, love, and experience all the joys of life if you don't put yourself back out there again. It takes courage...a lot of courage...but it's worth it.

There are three levels of trust. It is possible to have all three, or to have only one or two. It is only possible to be truly happy when all three are in place.

1. Trust in self: You make your own decisions, use your intuition, talk to others but don't rely on others to make decisions for you.

2. Trust in others: Everyone has 100% trust until they prove untrustworthy. You believe all people are good inside.

3. Trust in the Universe: You know you are part of a bigger plan, so even when things seem wrong, you know they will improve.

An honest frown is worth more than a million phony smiles. Pretending to be happy in an attempt to not disappoint others will only leave everyone unhappy in the end. Expressing feelings honestly is the only way to resolve differences and create truly happy surroundings.

If a friend stops speaking with you because they believed gossip about you without even asking you "your side," then you didn't really lose a friend. You only lost a person who didn't trust or believe in you...and that's not really a loss at all. It hurts because it feels unfair, and you would not have treated them the same way. But if that's the choice they've made, you can really only accept it and let them go. Even if you convince them this time, the absence of trust will not have changed, and will continue to hurt you in every future circumstance.

Someone else's insecurity and mistrust are the roots of big time drama. You can expect to spend a lot of time explaining, justifying, coddling, and walking on eggshells if you choose to be close to someone who struggles with those things. With your best efforts and patience, you may be able to help them some, but only they can fix themselves. If it's turning you into a nervous wreck then even though you'd love to help, you may have to set that ideal down and take care of yourself by creating some distance. It just may be that distance becomes the signal to them that they need to change if they want to keep a great person around.

Communication is important. Otherwise, the most you have to go by are actions and assumptions. If it's important to you, make an extra effort to talk to the person or people directly. Then use your intuition and logic to make sense of the whole thing. You can't make a whole decision on partial information.

Rebuilding trust when it's been broken is not dependent only on the person who has broken it, or how many times they can prove they will be honest. It depends on the person who has had their trust broken. If they choose to trust again and if they are able to, the relationship may be worth another try. If they are not able to trust again at all and would be in a constant panicked or anxious emotional state, the relationship has no hope of survival and should be ended.

The worst thing about lies is that they cause a person to doubt if they should trust so much. But the problem isn't too much trust, the problem is too many lies. Recognize when you can't trust a certain person anymore but don't let that spill over to all people. You'll never find true love at arm's length, but if you put up a wall of mistrust, that's the closest anyone can get.

Opening yourself up to a person takes a huge amount of courage and trust. Even if you think you know, you never really know how they will react or respond and that will always be out of your control. In keeping them out, you keep the risk of disappointment and pain out. But in keeping them out, you keep the chance of acceptance and love out, too. In the end, you really have to decide if the risk or the chance is more important to you and act accordingly.

Always assume that people cannot understand your perspective and feelings unless you've explained them to them. What is so clear from where you stand may be completely invisible from a different perspective.

If you do explain and they still don't get it or just don't care, then it doesn't mean you've wasted your time. It just means that you now know for sure that if you value being understood or considered, this won't be a person who can do those things very well if even at all.

An apology doesn't come with an eraser. Forgiveness doesn't mean memory loss. Once the house of trust is broken, it has to be rebuilt. Things aren't the way they were before, and they may not be for some time.

If the person who wasn't truthful isn't willing to be patient and open to rebuild broken trust then it may not be possible to rebuild.

5. Appreciation

When people we love (or pets) are in our life, we see them as healthy and here, because that is what they are in this moment. Yet at some point, they will not be in our lives. They may choose to leave, or they may pass away. If you were given a list of how long you had left with each relationship, would you appreciate more the ones you will have for the shortest amounts of time? We do not know how much time we have. All we are guaranteed is this moment. Make sure everyone who is important to you knows it every single day.

Appreciation is the basis for holidays, but it's something that can and should be done every day. Think of each holiday and what it means. Then, look around you and appreciate all the good that is in your life. Your family, friends, possessions, where you live. If you focus on what is good, more good will come. If you focus on what is lacking, soon, more will be lacking. Anything that is focused on increases, so the more you appreciate what you have, the more you will have to appreciate!

Sometimes when we do good things, believe in people, or try our hardest, we seem to get nothing in return...not even a "thank you." While this can be very disheartening, please don't ever think it was a waste of time. By putting good out into the world, you have done your part in making it a better place. Maybe you were not appreciated immediately, but maybe one day that person will look back and realize how kind you were to them. Maybe. Until then, please accept a sincere, "Thank you" from me on their behalf.

Appreciation for what you have doesn't mean you have to resign thinking anything could be even better. Appreciative and complacent are two different words. Being appreciative while striving to improve will allow you to be happy every step of the way.

If you're tired of being let down, put down, or brought down by the same person or people, maybe it's time to quit giving them any more opportunities to do so. Maybe it's time to create some room in your life for a person or people who value you.

While it's true that no one can "make you" feel any certain thing, good or bad, that doesn't mean that there's something wrong with you if what others say or do affects you. We are human beings after all, and the only reason we walk, talk, and learned to use the potty was because someone encouraged us to do so. Harsh environments grow much fewer flowers. Limit the time you spend in them when possible, shake it off as best you can, and really try to make quality time with those who value you. Make sure not to damper your quality time by talking too much about those others that affect you negatively. Enjoy your quality time and the effects of those others will diminish on their own.

Everything in the world has a natural ebb and flow. The tides move out but flow in again. While the flow is much more comfortable, the ebb has great meaning. When time and resources are stripped away, you can see clearly what and who truly matters to you and who you matter to in return. When your flow returns, you'll know exactly with who and where your time will be best spent, with a brand new appreciation for it all.

Appreciating a lesson learned means being grateful you have the wisdom for tomorrow that you didn't have yesterday.

6. Love

Love means, "I accept you as you are, exactly as you are. It does not mean that you are perfect, but it does mean that every single thing about you is 100% acceptable. Many things are even more than just acceptable, they are wonderful! But there is absolutely nothing you need to change in order to become loveable."

The moment you believe these things about yourself, you have found true love. You are then open to share it with another person who feels the same way.

When you touch someone's heart, they will never quite be the same again. Part of your life will live in them, always.

Others will treat you exactly as you treat yourself. Once you love yourself, you will not be able to tolerate poor treatment. You will be able to see that although they may call it love, it's actually something else.

"Do unto others as you'd have done to you" also means "do unto yourself as you would do to others." If someone is treating you poorly, just don't allow it. You would not do that to someone else. If they continue, remove yourself from that relationship. They may not even be capable of treating others well, but that you can't fix.

If someone doesn't accept you now, it's likely they won't accept you later, either. Don't change for anyone. Even if you change everything they've complained about, they'll just make up a new list of things for you to work on. Having a discussion and being honest with each other can do more than just salvage a relationship, it can save it. What is it that you don't like about each other? Be open. Can you each accept those things even if you'd prefer them to be different? If the answer is no, then realize that it will be a repeating argument. Even if people make promises to change and even if they really want to, it still takes time. No sense both of you being unhappy in the meantime about things that may or may not ever change. That "meantime" could be a whole lifetime away.

There's a big difference between giving someone the benefit of the doubt and turning a blind eye to anything someone does just because you like them a lot. Being generous and understanding are great qualities, just make sure someone doesn't use them all up on you. Kindness should be appreciated, not taken advantage of.

Loving and supporting someone is not the same as loving and supporting someone's actions if they are harming themselves or others. The first, encourages, the second, enables.

It takes courage to say, "I love you, but I can't support what you're doing." But that will give them incentive to change much more than hoping they'll change ever will.

Easier said than done, but better done than only wished for.

The more confident you are, the less need you'll feel to defend yourself against criticism. The more secure you are, the less insults will hurt. The more self worth you have, the less time you'll waste on those who don't see much in you. So put your energy into recognizing and developing yourself, your talents, your wellbeing, and you'll find that your closest relationships support you, and in turn you support them, too. The good times will be richer and the hard times will be more manageable. Life will be filled with love.

There are two things you should never be afraid of when resolving a disagreement with someone you love; to tell them when you think that they are wrong, and to admit to them when you believe that they are right. Neither will be easy to do at first, but both will ultimately build greater trust between you and a deeper love and respect.

Some people think that if they always assume the best in people and their intentions, that's "being positive," but it's really not. Now, it's not good to assume the worst, either. Just don't assume anything. Ask. Observe. Ask again. Observe again.

If you only assume the best, you will eventually be disappointed when you realize that they are not who they never were.

If you ask and observe, you can truly get to know them, and choose to accept them as they really are, with no false pedestals and no expectations of perfection.

That's "being positive."

In fact, that's love.

Set your heart free. Trust it. It knows the way. The way is always detached, secure, and out of love. Detachment doesn't mean coldness, it means freedom. Security doesn't mean rules or checking up on people, it means confidence and trust. Love doesn't mean clinging or desperation, it means appreciation, encouragement, and peace within.

The emotion paves the road to the destination. If you act out of love, you'll end up in a place of love, even though there may be some bumps or changing of roles in between here and then.

For example, acting with envy will not lead to a good place once that thing or person is won. There will just be more envy about something else.

Like an actor, ask yourself, "What's my motivation?"

Make sure that anger or other places you don't want to end up don't motivate your choices or decisions. Those negative emotions tend to begin as reactions to getting hurt, and can only survive once fed with more reasons to continue.

If healing is allowed to take place, those emotions can be let go. Moving forward in life can be done from a place of peace, of happiness, and of love. Even though it may not be a sunshine ride along the way over a candy-coated rainbow, the end destination when responding to life with these emotions will be a rewarding and loving location that could not have been reached any other way.

Looking for love can feel like searching for a missing piece of your heart. You will keep looking for that one special person who will complete you, until you finally realize that person is you. It's better to share a full heart with another person, rather than one that has a piece missing that they can never fill.

Decide that your goal is to love your whole life. Look at what's preventing that from being true and what already allows it. Plan for better days and work towards them. Use "yes" and "no" more and more to reflect your true feelings, not what you think everyone wants to hear.

Love is natural. When we do not act out of love, it goes against our very nature. That choice results in emotional, mental, and even physical pain. Love heals the pain that was caused by the absence of it. Always act out of love.

True love can't be planned or reasoned. It can only be felt and nourished with more love.

You cannot receive true love until you love yourself first. We see only a reflection of ourselves in other people. You will only accept the love that you feel inside. If you don't love yourself, you will think it's love when someone treats you poorly, even though in your mind you may know you should be treated better. If you were treated better, you would lose interest because it would not match the feeling you have inside. We reject anything more than we feel we truly deserve. Love yourself, accept yourself, and you will no longer be attracted to those who don't treat you with love and kindness. Feel love, receive love.

Look for beauty in ordinary things and your world will become amazing.

No matter how long it takes, true love is always worth the wait. If you are with someone just to be with someone, then you won't be available when the right someone comes along. Fear of being alone is a subconscious fear that you alone are not whole, not enough, not love in and of yourself. That energy will come across as desperation and will lead to a relationship with someone either very needy or very controlling. Neither of those are love. Feeling whole and complete alone but being open to a loving relationship will be the exact right energy to begin and foster a beautiful connection. And no matter if it happens early in life or later in life, nothing will be missed and no time wasted. Certain qualities take time to develop, cannot be rushed, and can only appreciated once they become complete.

Love between two people is a free flow of giving and receiving. Love given but not received leads to resentment, depletion, lowered self-worth, and feeling used. Love received but not given leads to feelings of guilt for not giving or not being able to give, and after that leads to unappreciation because it came so easily and stayed for no reason.

Either way, love that exists in only one form or the other but not both causes deep pain. True love then knows enough to realize when it must love enough to let go.

True love isn't blind. It sees imperfections but doesn't let them obstruct the view.

You don't have to know someone to love them. You don't even have to be in a relationship with someone to love them. Every single person you see, even total strangers are worthy of love. They were once a tiny infant, an entire lifetime ahead of promise. Where they are today, that depends on what has happened to them since. They may be destitute, living on the street. Love them for their determination to carry on each day regardless of having very little reason to do so. Or they could be a tyrant of a boss, driven by money and achievement. Love them and hope they achieve more and more because eventually, they'll realize it never really mattered and will see how much life passed them by in their pursuits. But by then it will be too late to go back and all of the things that could have mattered will be gone or have moved on. Send them a silent thought of love because one day, they will need it. In every meeting and every goodbye, think silently, "I love you" to each person. They won't hear it, but they will feel it, and you will feel at peace and connected more than you could imagine.

"Love heals" isn't just a wishful thought. Love literally heals a broken heart, dashed hopes, and shattered faith. It gives rise to new dreams out of old ones that were not fulfilled. It sees the importance of the individual, of the moment, and also of the bigger picture at the very same time. It brings peace to tragedy and calm to chaos. It does not erase the hurt, but it always makes it better than it could ever possibly be without it.

Love means acceptance, kindness, encouragement, and care. With love, doubt disappears, fears fade, and there's a comfort that develops which makes even being alone a place of solace. You'll help to heal and inspire others just by being yourself. You'll help them discover that it's possible for them, too. It's a beautiful gift.

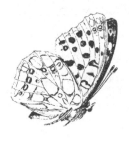

7. Thoughts and Words

Our thoughts are always true to our feelings. We, and only we, know for certain what they are. Before they become words, they may turn into what we think others would like to hear, but our thoughts do not change. Others can only assume that our words are our thoughts, and will react and respond to our words alone. This is why it's so important to always speak true to your thoughts. Others may not approve or agree with what you say. To speak your truth takes courage, but it is essential to relationships built on honesty and trust.

If you always want to say the right thing, make sure to always think the right thoughts. Someone who wants to make a good impression, but has worried thoughts about making a bad impression, will likely say things that come out wrong, that they didn't mean that way, or that they shouldn't have said at all. Your thoughts are your word generators. By keeping your mind calm and confident, everything you say will come out just fine.

Be aware of your words as you say them. Words are so very powerful, and we never know what state of mind someone is in at any time. You choose your words, but you cannot choose the affect they will have on people. Always speak out of love. True power does not crush others, but helps them to see their own greatness.

Sometimes, words are better left unsaid. Other times, those unspoken words could make all the difference in the world.

If you look for positives, you will see only positives, and be blind to negatives that may hurt you later. If you look for only negatives, you will find only them, and be blind to positives that you may love. It's only when you look, just look, that you can see things as they really are. It's only when you clearly see both positives and negatives that you can accurately decide if this certain experience is one you want in your life, or not.

If you found out, realized, or learned something today that totally changes how you would have acted, or decisions you made in the past, don't beat yourself up for not knowing it before. Think instead of how much your life will change from this day forward, now that you know it, and how much better and wiser your decisions will be in the future. Be grateful that you learned it today, and not ten years from now.

Old habits die hard, but if you know the results and don't want to see them anymore, you've got to change the choices that keep leading up to them. The more they've happened, the easier it is to recognize a pattern. Most times, you need to be able to see a pattern before you can tell what it is you need to change. Maybe you didn't see it the first time or the fifth time or the twenty-seventh time but things aren't always all that clear. The important thing is to change it when you do recognize it. When you do, your whole life from now on will change for the better. Don't look back with regret. Look forward with the promise of brighter days ahead.

Your mind wants to be right, but your soul wants the truth. This is why you should never discuss conflicting ideas in anger or sadness. Anger and sadness are emotions of the mind. When faced with the truth that your soul recognizes, you will feel it in your heart, but with the anger or sadness, your mind will force you to keep arguing, find something else to be right about, or deny being wrong. This prevents the truth and peace from returning.

Reality is nothing more than your beliefs mixed with your experiences. In reality, there are as many worlds as there are people, as no two of us have an identical set of beliefs and experiences. We may be similar to some, and to others, we may be near opposites. No one is wrong, and no one is right. We are all just living true to what we think we know. If someone says, "be realistic" in the face of your dreams, there's no need to become angry, or to try to convince them of your view. Stay true to yourself, be positive, and watch your reality improve.

Think for a moment about the meanings of the words, "encouraging," and "discouraging." Courage is carrying on, regardless of the presence of fear. To en-courage someone is to enable them to have the courage to continue in the direction they are going. To dis-courage someone is to disable them from having courage. One kind word, or one unkind word, could be the one thing that kept someone going, or the last straw that made them quit. Be aware of this when you choose which words you give to people.

If someone says they will do one thing, but then they do the opposite, you have two choices:

1. Assume why

2. Ask why

They may have a logical answer, but you'll never really know unless you ask.

Assuming the worst in a person hurts them. Assuming the best in a person disappoints you. Assuming nothing allows you both the ability to see the truth.

Viewing rejection as "you're not good enough" will cause you to try to change in order to become "good enough" for that person or circumstance. Seeing rejection as "it's not right for you, but they happened to recognize it first," frees you to find something or someone who is right for you instead.

At the heart of this shift in thinking are four very important things:

Love yourself

1. Accept yourself

2. Do your best

3. Have confidence in the other three.

There's a big difference between just feeling sorry for yourself and reflecting on your feelings. If you can't talk to anyone openly about then, then journal. If you don't know what's wrong, you can't fix it. Reflection is essential. Write down what you're feeling, what seems to be causing the draining and depressing feelings, and think in terms of how you're contributing to the circumstances (even if only by allowing them to continue) and what you can do to change them. It takes effort, but it's worth it.

Resolve to remain humble enough that every honest compliment or thank you is a surprise, received with appreciation. Resolve to remain hopeful enough that every disappointment is a surprise, received with acceptance from that person, but never extended to be expected from all people.

Every thought, every spoken word, every action sets a process in motion. We control what we send out, but not the results or consequences that follow. Good intentions set forth with the goal to destroy a perceived wrong will cause destruction in their wake. Good intentions set forth in love will yield good results, eventually. Be conscious of method even when certain of intentions.

In all your waking hours, you're having a mind party. Your thoughts are your guests. Those which you don't pay attention to and refuse to entertain will eventually get bored and leave. Make sure to only entertain the ones that you want to keep around.

There's a big difference between "focusing on negative things" and "ignoring something that needs some attention for it to be resolved." Always remember the teaching mantra, "what you allow, you encourage."

Bottling up painful emotions eventually turns them all into a prison of anger and sadness. Expressing them releases them and frees your soul. It may feel awkward and vulnerable at first, but after some practice it becomes easier and feels so much better than holding them all inside.

The longer you believe, "that's just how it is," the longer it will be that way. In fact, you'll have no reason to even explore other possibilities because there would seem to be no point. When you believe in better, brighter, more amazing possibilities, they begin to open up in front of you. Not all right away, not often the way you planned, but the path of discovery will only exist when you believe it does. And belief is always a choice.

What you impress people by is what you are impressed by in other people. If you are impressed by kindness and generosity, that means those things are in you and you believe they are important. Those who are impressed by displays of status, power, flash, or waving money around don't yet see the value in the qualities those actions show are lacking in that person...humility and gratitude. If a person doesn't value your good qualities, it doesn't mean they're not important. They're just not important to that person, and probably not present in them because of that.

Energy and time are limited life resources. Be conscious of where you spend them so that there is more than enough of both for the things and people who are most important to you.

Physical beauty is only skin deep but the beauty of the soul is infinite.

Those who order up a big plate of dishonesty will find that it comes with a side order of regret. No substitutions. In the end, you'll never regret not doing the wrong thing. You will always be glad you did the right thing, maybe not sooner, but definitely later on.

An open mind to brighter possibilities opens doors that decades of experience thought for certain were locked.

Behind each set of eyes lives another wandering soul who, under different circumstances, could have been you.

8. Power

Before you get or achieve what you believe you want, it's really only an ideal. Everything has positive and negative to it. When you have nothing, there's nothing to lose...and there's a freedom in that. When you have more, there is more to lose. Develop security not in things but in yourself, your abilities, resilience, adaptability and determination. This will far greater surpass any comfort achieved in any thing or relationship that exists outside of yourself.

The word "power" has many definitions, but one that it has become attached to is one that is negative. All "power" means is concentrated energy. A lot of energy without focus or concentration is just static, and serves little purpose. But focused energy becomes power, which can change people, circumstances, and situations worldwide. You have great power. When you use your power to initiate, whether it be a bowling league, or cleaning up a neighborhood, others are attracted to it, and the power increases.

True power is shown by how many people one has helped in their lifetime, not how many one has hurt. It takes power to drown the hopes of others, but it ends there. Using that power instead to help others swim to shore will cause them to help others because of you. The world with you in it will be a slightly worse or slightly better place. You, and only you, can determine your legacy.

If someone spends time going out of their way to harm others, it's really sad. It means they have no clue how precious and brief their life really is. Don't waste any of your life being angry with them. To do so would be giving them power over your happiness. They will regretfully prove to be their own worst enemy.

With a few chosen words, we have the power to either make someone's day or to ruin it.

Staying quiet to keep the peace can be a good thing, but if the peace has already been disturbed, staying quiet won't make anything better.

Summon your courage and speak up when you feel the need to.

People will either encourage you to fly or sit on your wings. Don't be a resting place for anyone's doubts or limitations. You've got places to go and you can't get to them standing still.

Feeling stuck in a situation is a very weakening experience. It may seem like due to finances or promises, obligations or loyalty, you cannot do anything but tolerate where you are. Over time, your heart will leave, your mind will leave, and only your body will remain. Though people may fear losing you, they really don't want to keep you if the only choice is to keep you there unhappily. If things can't be fixed or made better, it is far more empowering for all involved to separate, but you may be the one who has to make that decision for the good of all.

Don't let something entirely out of your control entirely control you.

When you really try to do right, to be positive, to be honest, and not many others seem to do the same or even care that you do, you may wonder "what's the point?" But that is the point. In your way, with your means, in your time here, you're making things better. No amount is too small but chances are the effect you have on people is much greater than you realize.

The mind has no time to dream of a better future if it's too busy chasing shadows from the past. Reflect, resolve, let go, live on.

Long overdue changes can happen very fast, but they still need decision and commitment to happen at all.

You cannot convince someone to see something that they do not want to see, or just cannot see, no matter how much you know it would improve their life. You have to love and accept them exactly as they are today. If you cannot do that, you have to let them go and find their own way, in their own time, if they ever choose to do so. Otherwise, you'll be giving them the power over your happiness, too.

When you try something new, you don't have to be perfect. In fact, you don't even have to be very good. If you love it, you'll want to do more of it, and you'll get better and better over time. A lot of people don't start things because they see how good other people are at doing them. But those other people probably weren't all that good when they first started, either. Talent is reserved for the few, but skill is open to anyone who takes the time to keep at something and make the effort to improve.

When afraid of facing their painful truth, some people will always run to something new and exciting, some people will always run to something old and familiar. But sooner or later, both will realize they are really running to nowhere until they finally face it and deal with it once and for all. Running may seem easier in the short term but it will end up leading to a lifetime of regret.

Courage takes forethought. You can feel awkward now for using it, or regretful later for not using it. There is some resistance in every chosen path, but the one that requires courage is usually the best one to choose. It leads to the real you. People talk often of taking the path of least resistance, but in the present moment it will always seem easier to avoid than deal with those awkward feelings. So it's best to think more in terms of choices and consequences and summon up that courage within. You won't regret it.

Don't stress about what you can't do. You can't always do the best thing, but you can always do your best. And that's much more than many choose to do.

You were born to be awesome. Don't let anyone talk you out of that. If anyone has and you believed them, don't believe it anymore. You were given gifts of talents and passions to use, not to remain throughout your life as idle potential. You've gained experiences and wisdom up to this point, and you'll use every single one. Become empowered and choose to really live all your life from now on. Discover your best life by heading in directions that nourish your soul. You don't need to know all the answers to start, they will reveal themselves as you go.

Circumstances that were out of your control put you where you started. Choices that are in your control get you where you end up.

Conflicting ideas are a part of life. We're all different and have different ideas and beliefs. But disagreements don't have to turn into arguments. Trying to avoid conflict at all costs by agreeing with everyone will wind up a giant, overwhelming mess with no one really knowing what's true and what's not. The best way to deal with conflict is to resolve it immediately with direct, open communication. Conflict resolution is a skill, but it can only be developed through practice. It's very hard at first and it can be tempting to just try and avoid it, but it gets easier and you get better at it the more you do it.

Becoming used to or numb to repeated emotional pain doesn't relieve it. It just makes you believe that life was meant to be barely tolerable. That's no way to live. Always believe life is a beautiful gift. If your surroundings don't support that, don't tolerate them for one second more than you absolutely have to.

Be aware of button pushing during disagreements. One common way that a person may attempt to sway your opinion is to introduce false isolation. That is, to say, "well everybody thinks what I think, and only you think differently." "Everybody" may be family, a group of friends, or just a made up "everybody" that doesn't really exist. If you react, not wanting to be the only one left out, then this method of persuasion will be used on you again and again. You will eventually lose confidence in your own thoughts. It usually comes after you ask for a reason. If there isn't a good one... "everybody else thinks so" seems to get pulled out as if that is a reason. But it's really not. Being aware of this allows you to respond and again ask for a reason, rather than just react and be persuaded against your own true feelings. It is good to be open to and consider other peoples opinions when things actually concern and affect them. But, be careful not to just abandon your own needs and concerns just because you've been told a group thinks otherwise...especially when decisions and outcomes don't even affect them. Every person has wants, needs, and opinions, and yours are just as valid and important as those of anyone else.

Tragedy shatters innocence but it need not destroy hope. Resolve to make things better, no matter the size of the result. The effort to improve is the key to a better tomorrow.

Maybe you don't have to push yourself forward.
Maybe you just have to stop holding yourself back.

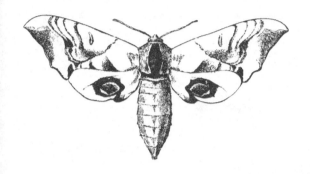

9. Time

Few of us have tons of "free" time. When we believe some-thing is important, we make time for it. Making time for the people who are most important in your life is crucial to happiness. A job can replace you, but to those who love you, you are irreplaceable. Prioritize your time with this in mind.

Time is never truly wasted. The point of life is to learn. Even if you were stuck in a bad relationship for a long, LONG time, it was the exact amount of time that was needed for the lesson. If when we were born, we received a guide to our lives that told us how long it would take to learn lessons about self-worth, changing people, and love, it would make things a lot easier, but it would be like a crossword book with all the words already circled. There just wouldn't be any point.

There's really no such thing as making up for lost time, but you can make the absolute most of the time you have now. Don't lose another moment to "should haves." Appreciate now, what's in front of you and what's coming in the days, weeks, and years ahead.

Time must be good at hiding. If you don't make an effort to find it, it sure will sneak up on you.

It does not matter how long a block of stone has existed. It does not matter how long a blank canvas rested on the ground. What turns these ordinary things into magnificent sculptures and paintings is talent, skill, and commitment by just one person who decides it's time. Recognize your own potential and use your talents and skills and commit to turning your life into the masterpiece it was meant to be. It's never too late to start. In fact, the older you are, the more skills you've acquired and the faster you will proceed. You just have to decide that it's time.

Time doesn't wait. Indecision will only let opportunities slip by. Pick a path and walk confidently with your heart behind every step.

If you were to travel back in time to younger days, you'd have to learn all that you've learned all over again. If you could fast forward to years from now, all of today's problems would be solved, all of the outcomes would be known, but the adventure would also be over. There would be no more choices left to make. So take that wisdom you've gained in all your past, live in the moment, do your best, summon your courage, and build your life on what you've learned. There is still time ahead of you, but it will pass quickly. Now is the time to do, to be, and to live.

It's not how much time you're given, it's what you do with the time you're given. Make the most of each day that you get.

Nothing is ever in stone until the moment passes. Once it does, only perspective can ever see it differently. And even stone erodes in time.

Eventually, most of it will make sense. The rest of it will have to be accepted for how it was. No better, no worse.

If you look at photos of yourself from five years ago, ten years ago, or more, you may feel a bit down comparing outer appearances. Yes, most likely, you look a little older now. But if you think of the person you were then compared to now, all the things you didn't know yet, the struggles you were going to have to make it through without knowing the outcome... Well maybe being here and now, knowing what you do now is worth a wrinkle or two. Someday you'll look back on photos of yourself today and think of how young you looked and how much more life lay ahead of you. So why not just make that someday today?

Every sunset is a curtain call to a day in the life of those who had the opportunity to live it. Challenges were met, smiles were exchanged, love was given. Do the best you can with each day because the show won't go on forever. Make sure each and every day, you give the performance of a lifetime.

We are here for a very short time. It's easy to get distracted or become so ingrained in habits that time seems to slip by faster than it really does. Once you realize you've not spent enough of your time where you wanted it to be, it's important to stay aware of where your minutes and hours are spent daily. Make your priorities into priorities instead of putting them off for some other time.

Being your best and trying your best are the same thing. The longer you try your best, the better you will become. Be patient, but persistent.

We each see the world through the filters of our pasts. This is how two sets of eyes can view the exact same thing but see it entirely differently.

The bloom may be brief but the memory of its beauty will last a lifetime. We are remembered by the beauty we leave behind.

There will never ever be another person like you, another day like this, another moment like this one. Make sure to appreciate the good in all three.

Do what you'll wish you would have done.

10. Faith

Faith means to believe something is true without having to see real proof. In fact, sometimes, faith means to believe something is true, regardless of what the "real" proof shows. If you have faith in a person, and it looks like, or you hear gossip that this person has done something wrong, you won't believe it until you hear it directly from them. Faith is tied to trust. You cannot have faith without trust, or trust without faith.

What's the difference between having faith and wishing? When you wish, you HOPE things will get better, but you may not BELIEVE they will. When you have faith, you BELIEVE things will get better, and you look for opportunities to make that happen. Think of the statements, "I wish you the best," versus, "I have faith you will succeed." Which is more confident? Don't just wish, have 100% faith!

It's hard sometimes to not be afraid. But it's much harder to always live in fear. Faith means to believe something is true, sometimes without any proof at all. Have faith in yourself and the proof will follow.

Shake it off, let it go, work through it. The more you do, the less there will be for you to have to carry around. Large or small, past or present, whatever is bringing you down. It's just too heavy to carry anymore. Decide what it all is, decide which way of release works best for you, and move forward. A brighter, lighter life ahead awaits you.

In something that's done and can't be changed, look only for the positives. In something that's current, look for the truth. You can't change your past but you sure can change your future. Look for what best serves both.

An honest, good intention with a poor method will lead to either frustration or learning one way that didn't work. A bad intention with a good method will lead to deception. Intention is one way or the other but method can be improved upon with the development of tact and consideration of different perspectives.

Conserving energy is a good thing. But this is also why belief is the root of all positive change. Unless you believe something better is possible, it makes no sense to devote the energy or effort into making it happen. So all those other things, determination, perseverance, courage....they can't do their jobs until their leader, belief, steps up front and center. Before you do anything, set your foundation firm in the belief that great things are very possible and that you are more than able to make them so.

Talk yourself into them, not out of them. It is a miracle that you are here right now and definitely against all rational odds. You have knowledge and experience.

If great things happen to other people, why wouldn't they happen to you?

Affirmations, prayer, meditation, use what works best to frame your mind that yes, yes, great things will be for you. Then set off in the direction that feels right. One step, one move, one day at a time.

A change in direction before it happens may seem like way too much work. But realize and remember momentum. Yes, it would take much less effort to continue on as is but if it isn't allowing you to feel good, to feel alive, or to wake up every day with positive anticipation then it has to change. If you really decide and commit, you'll find the time, energy, and courage to make changes. Even really big changes. And they may be incredibly challenging and cause all sorts of doubts to fire up within and you may at times wish you hadn't even bothered. But just when you've given it your best and things don't look too much different, you'll find that momentum has kicked in...but this time in the direction that you truly want to go. From there it will become easier and yet easier to continue. You'll wonder why you waited so long to begin.

The road from bad to good often has a little stretch of awful in between. It takes a whole lot of courage to face and go through the awful stretch, but it will be totally worth it when you do.

When you believe, when you put in the hours, when you do your best work, when you keep going, eventually, you'll find that luck has very little to do with your success. It starts with a dream, but a dream has to become your life for your life to become that dream fully realized. You can totally do it. Start where you are and commit to getting to where you want to be.

Some puzzles only make sense once the very last piece is in place. Before then, all best efforts, hopes, and beliefs seem to be going to dead ends. Faith will carry you through to the last piece. Keep going. No matter what, keep going ~ doing what you can and what feels right to your heart.

It's a big job, shortening the distance between wanting and believing. The closer they are together, the more likely the reality will be. But don't force yourself. Forcing causes anxiety and a feeling of being overwhelmed. That energy pushes away good things and sheds doubt on good beliefs. Encourage yourself. Nudge yourself. Stretch just a little further every day. Go at your pace and build your confidence gradually and your positive changes will be solid. Breathe deeply and take those steps. You can do it.

Desperate times do not require desperate measures, they require stronger faith.

People wonder how they can have faith when there seems to be no reason to have any. But that is the most important reason to have it. A belief is the spark, but it alone cannot sustain. It must be nourished with faith in order to grow and remain. The strength of positive beliefs and faith will lead to energy, opportunities, openmindedness, and possibilities that just would not exist without them.

The only thing you should give up is wondering if you should just give up. Don't waste your time and energy on doubts. You'll need as much of both of them as you have to stay motivated to get through.

Maybe it's not that easy, but maybe it's not that difficult either. Every moment is possible. Moments become days, and days become years. Looking back, you'll wonder how you made it. How you made it through an impossible time. You'll have done it moment by precious, possible moment.

11. Self Worth

Some people will like you for no reason, some people will not like you for no reason. Who you choose to spend the most time, thoughts, and effort on, depend on exactly how much you like yourself. By just staying near to people who treat you poorly, you are telling them it's OK to do so. Only keep people close to you who treat you well.

Sometimes your greatest teachers in life had no idea just what they taught you. Especially those who treated you the worst. The day you said, "I deserve better than this." was the day you graduated from their class.

When you are doing well, some people, even friends and family members, won't be happy for you. It's due to envy. A person only envies when they feel the same is not possible for themselves. This is due to low self-esteem and low self-confidence. It has nothing to do with you, and you should never feel you need to dim your light because someone else doesn't realize theirs could shine just as brightly. When you shine, you will become an object of envy to some, but you will inspire many others.

Many people believe they are "too nice" and that is why they get treated poorly over and over. Remember the Golden Rule, "Do unto others as you'd have done to you." If you treated someone poorly, would you expect them to just put up with it? Of course not, so you shouldn't put up with it, either. Being "too nice" to someone who treats you poorly is not a sign that you love them very much, but rather a sign that you don't love yourself enough. You are worthy of more.

If you really want an answer, stop asking,

"Why am I being treated this way?"

and ask instead,

"Why am I putting up with this?"

p.s. It's not "love."

Building, or rebuilding, self worth after the break up of a damaging relationship starts with stopping the negative thoughts of the one who is no longer there, and thinking positive thoughts of the one who still is...you.

People who have had low self worth for a long time cannot just be confident one day. Habits need to change gradually. You do know that you would not stand by and let someone treat your best friend or your child poorly. So when someone is treating you poorly, stop and think of what you would tell your best friend or child to say in those moments, and use that great advice for yourself.

Compassion dissolves anger. Understanding why someone behaves the way they do allows for forgiveness when they have mistreated you. Maybe they are insecure, or in pain, or maybe they even suffered some type of abuse in their lifetime, and you can see why they are the way they are. But when your compassion extends to excusing them for treating you poorly, over and over, it not only damages your self worth, but prevents them from healing as well. Refuse to allow it to continue, for everyone's sake.

It's hard to rebuild self worth, and it's even harder when they people around you keep on putting you down, belittling your ambitions, and telling you that you're not good enough. But if everyone suddenly cheered on your every move, you wouldn't know which insults still bothered you. For an insult to bother you, you have to agree with it. Otherwise, you can dismiss it as nonsense. Though those people make it harder, they're also indirectly showing you the areas within you that still need to be rebuilt.

Have you ever heard someone say one thing and then do another and asked them why? You may have been shocked at their reaction.

"Don't judge me! What are you accusing me of? How dare you ask me that?!" and immediately began to apologize for asking, as your intention was none of those things. You just didn't know why they said one thing and did another.

Sometimes, it's just a sensitive subject. Other times, many times, the reaction comes from them judging themselves, being afraid of being caught in a lie, or trying to hide something.

Stay aware, and realize that if you can't freely communicate, this may not be a healthy friendship or relationship for you.

An enormous benefit of having self worth is that a person can accept a compliment gratefully, knowing inside that it's true. Sincere compliments feel good, just as they are intended to feel. Without self worth, a person can only reject or barely half accept a compliment, while deep inside they may wish in sadness that they could truly believe it. Compliments are not supposed to hurt.

There are two paths to self-worth.

One begins with a real or perceived lack of support, love, or encouragement in childhood. As the child becomes an adult, he or she has to decide to have something which was never fostered or nurtured. This is difficult to overcome because there is a false belief that if one's parents didn't love them, the two people who should have the most and knew them the most, then how could anyone who truly knew them, love them? Challenges are: letting people in, becoming comfortable with the vulnerability that is love.

The second path to self-worth begins with a real or perceived abundance of support, love, or encouragement in childhood. As the child becomes an adult, he or she is accustomed to being loved, approved of, and validated within the home. When this person is rejected, it's so completely foreign to them that they may be drawn in to try to prove their worth to this job, friend, or relationship. They cannot understand why they are not loved. Challenges are: realizing rejection doesn't mean that there's a need to change the self to become acceptable to another, discovering worth that is independent of the agreement or disagreement of others.

Neither path is easy. Neither path is impossible to navigate.

It may take a few of the same relationship to occur before a pattern is recognized. Even then, if the person comes to the conclusion that "all women are emotional" or "all men are liars" then they are missing their lesson.

If, and only if, they recognize their part in allowing the mistreatment to continue and assessing the reasons why, will they be freed from the obstacle of lack of self-worth.

The pitfall is to become trapped in wonder if their childhood had only been different. No matter how it had been, there would still be the "other side" to face within adult relationships. Challenges to self-worth would either arise in the form of "that's all I've ever known" or "I've never experienced this before."

Be patient, but persistent in building or rebuilding your self worth. The path to self-worth can only be reached when you love and accept yourself. Not only "when you're perfect," but right now, today, exactly as you are. Accepting yourself will not mean you will lose the drive to become better. It is the opposite. You have to believe in someone to believe they can become more than who they appear to be today. Otherwise, it would seem like a waste of effort.

You were not stupid for getting into and stuck in bad relationships and situations, you just didn't love yourself enough or see your worth. Forgive your younger self for thinking so little of you. From now on, move forward in life, with love for yourself and aware of your worth. This will give you the ability to walk away from those who, for whatever reason, just don't see it.

Don't let the worse people get the best of you. Save it for the best people instead. If a mean person doesnt like you for no reason, remember this:

Your purpose here on Earth is not to try to win the approval of mean people.

If someone asks you to do more and you have a big reaction inside, it may be a sign that you're already doing too much. Even strong, independent, hard-working people have limits and deserve to rest. Doing your best is a wonderful thing, but doing all you possibly can for as long as you possibly can will eventually lead to burning out and feeling unappreciated by the people around you.

Sometimes people confuse self-love with big ego. The two are totally different. A person with a big ego thinks they are better than others. A person who loves him or herself doesn't think they are better or worse than others. Comparing is useless, as we all have strengths and weaknesses. Focusing on one or the other is not the whole picture. If you love yourself, you know you are worthy of love, of good things in life, and that you are capable of unlimited great things. You will inspire others to realize the same about themselves as well.

The more you see your own worth, the less you care about the opinions of people who don't value you much, and the more you are able to appreciate those who do.

They're called 2nd chances, not 342nd chances. Never giving up on someone else usually means giving up on yourself somewhere along the way. Don't live on the whims or indecision of someone you really care about. At a certain point, it's time to move on.

When you try to make things better for a lot of people, you may end up making things worse for yourself. A little self-sacrifice is noble, but depriving yourself of too much will only leave you depleted. By that time, most people won't even realize that you need anything, because you're the one who has always given. Take care of yourself. Self preservation is not selfish, it's essential for living a full and happy life.

The freedom to be yourself is a gift only you can give yourself. But once you do, no one can take it away.

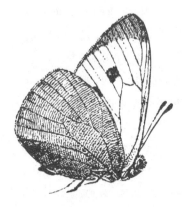

12. Happiness

Happiness is really nothing more than freedom; freedom to love, to be yourself, and to live without fear of change. There are times when happiness would be incredibly difficult. Physical pain, mental and emotional challenges can be all but overwhelming. But even in those times, to find just a moment of peace provides the strength to carry on.

Later on in life, we're not the same as we once were. We've had our hearts broken, faced disappointments and tragedies but made it through. This time is likely the most beautiful outside of infancy. Though we are weary travelers with far less energy than before, we still carry within us a spark of hope and a great deal of love. It is with focus and this energy that we can truly live a life fulfilled.

The only outcome you can be certain of is the one that happened. It may seem like if only you'd done something differently or if only someone else would have, then things would be better than they are today. But thinking that way will leave you disappointed with your life as it turned out. More than likely, if one thing had been different, it would not have led to a much more wonderful life than you have now. What people thought was important or not at the time would still have been the same. People were how they were, knew what they knew, cared about what they cared about, and did what they did. Given those things, this is the only outcome that was ever really possible. And you know, if you look at what could have happened but didn't, the good choices you made, and that you realized things when you did and not years later in life, then now as it is ~exactly as it is~ becomes a pretty good place after all.

To take the path of least resistance does not mean to offer no resistance to anything that comes across your path. It means to be aware of your options in life, think on their consequences both immediate and future, and act on those which feel best to your soul.

They may not be perfect for everyone, and others may try to steer your path in the direction that they prefer. It is up to you what you choose.

Consider those who you love in your choices, but if your choices conflict with their expectations of you, then you have to decide if

1. trying to be who they want you to be, or

2. being who you really are

is ultimately more important to everyone's long term happiness. You can only pretend for so long, but you can be yourself until your very last breath.

Changing our own lives takes work. It takes courage, patience, persistence, and the strength to continue to be positive about those changes no matter how slow they may appear to be going. But it's worth it.

The energy of change builds up and can be used to do this.

Unfortunately, that courage thing can easily prevent people from going forward. What doesn't take courage is to look at someone else's life and pick out all their perceived flaws and criticize them at random. Maybe this is why people do that so often instead of working on their own lives.

You don't have to be the same. Use your energy to better your own life and keep your attention on it. If you're being criticized by someone or even by a few people, don't waste too much energy trying to explain things to them or to defend your choices or fill them in on all they don't know.

You need all your energy to continue working on yourself.

Our very survival depends on the ability to filter out the overwhelming amount of information that all our senses are receiving at any given moment.

Being conscious of thought and of feelings is not the normal state of most people, but it is a very possible and peaceful place to be.

Practice focusing your attention on peaceful and grateful thoughts, affirmations or just re-appreciating any and every good thing that's in your life right now. We can only process so much. We can only give our attention and energy to so much.

A mind full of worry has no room for hope. A mind full of doubt has no room for confidence. A mind full of gratitude sees no lack. A mind full of curiosity, love, humor, and goodness will always manage to deal with adversity as it comes but returns to the habit-formed state of peace.

Like any habit, it takes at first a lot of conscious energy and effort, but soon becomes the natural state of being. It's a wonderful goal to achieve.

When each day starts, decide it's going to be a good day. Decide to be happy. As the day goes on, whenever something happens that prevents it, decide if you'll continue to carry that thing throughout the day or if you can set it down and continue on. Traffic, a disappointment, an unexpected bill, a snide remark...decide if any of those things are more important than the happiness of the day, and if not, give them only as much attention as is needed and carry on.

It takes awhile to figure out who you are, what you need and want and what you don't. Up to two-thirds of life is spent just figuring out these basic things. Because of the time invested in that process, the last third of your life will be ridiculously amazing. Life has only just begun. Live it to the fullest.

Our attention spans may have been caught up in the pressures of chasing faster, bigger, more, and new, but our souls have known all along that achievement of any of those things brings only temporary satisfaction. Then, the race begins again. They do not bring happiness. Happiness is found in looking at what you have right here, right now, and feeling at peace and appreciative of it all. Striving to improve is an excellent pursuit as long as it doesn't take away from the fulfillment of the present moment. Those who find happiness at every step won't have a need for any top. Those who will only be happy at the top will only seek a new top once they arrive there.

Wake up and be awesome. Keep dreaming. Don't be afraid to love, it's what we're all here for. Do what's in your heart and you won't have nearly as many regrets. Have the courage to disappoint people if it means being honest, because they value your honesty more than your half-hearted approval. Things won't always be fair, or right, but act as if you were a billion people and have faith that the good you do matters. Every little light brightens up the world, and the only one you can ever shine is your own. Shine bright, do right, love on.

When you feel you've failed at something, it can be anywhere from discouraging to devastating. The last thing you want to do is try again. All that effort and it ended in a huge disappointment.

But nothing in its entirety is ever a failure.

For a time, it brought you happiness, nourished your hope, and there were many, many good moments.

Nothing in life is permanent; not even life is permanent. So take up those good memories with you and move forward. If you only remember the pain, if you only remember the end, you'll have a dark fog around you that will prevent you from seeing all the opportunities and new beginnings that come your way every single day.

Lift the fog and face every new day with optimism. Sure, there's bound to be some more trying times ahead, but there will be many amazing times, too.

You're here to love and learn, and at those two things, you have always, always succeeded.

Made in the USA
Las Vegas, NV
16 July 2021

26527367R00059